"Norma's faith is infectious ...w years, I have spent many an hour hearing the stories in this book, and, no matter how I felt before, I always came away encouraged and with a bigger view of God. Reading this book will leave you with greater faith and expectation that God is alive and working in our world today and wants to be at work in your life too."

—Pastor John Gridley

"Norma is one of the most faith-filled and discerning people I have ever met. One day, some time ago, she mentioned to me that, in the previous week, the Lord had given her the numbers to win the national lottery. I believed her. But when I asked her how much she had won, she said that the Lord had not told her to buy a ticket. I bet she has a lot more stories like that."

—John Price

"I have known Norma and Sarath for over 20 years; their home has become my home away from home. Norma has been my spiritual mother, teacher, encourager, and friend over the last 20 years. She has invested many hours of teaching and prayer time in my life and others and has always reminded me that my treasure can only be found in the face of God. I thank God for her faithfulness and dedication and using her enormous talents for His glory, and for freely sharing *the richness of her sweet and godly spirit. Thank you, Norma, for your continuous prayers and love which has kept me steadfast through the years. I pray God's goodness and mercy follow you all the days of your life."*

—Sherena Simon

"I remember the first time I met Norma. She was sat next to her husband, Sarath, and our church service had just finished. I noticed her smiling at us. First thing that came to my mind: this is a woman who knows her God. A woman who has so much to say about Jesus in her life. She had the testimony of Jesus in her life. And I just wanted to sit and listen to the revelation of God in her life and her family's life. I wasn't wrong; Norma absolutely loves her God despite everything that life throws at her."

—Viniana Vunivalu

"I have never met a godlier person than Norma. She believes in the Lord, and He always hears her prayers. Whenever she or her husband were ill, the Lord always prompted me to call them. Now when she is ill, I call her and pray for her. She inspires me. All her conversations are God-based and about His goodness. May all who read these testimonies be blessed and inspired. In these God reveals His goodness to His children."

— Ethel Haymer

the FAITHFULNESS of God

the FAITHFULNESS of God

A Collection of Testimonies

Norma Alahendra

Alahendra Publishing

To my beloved Sarath who went on to glory whilst I was writing this book.

I miss you so much.

There is such a void in my life.

CONTENTS

FOREWORD

In her long and varied life, Norma Alahendra has maintained a steadfast faith. Raised in a Christian home in Sri Lanka, she has never wavered in her trust in Jesus, despite many ups and downs along the way. She has many testimonies of the power of prayer in her life, and in the life of her family, and, in this book, Norma tells these stories in a lively and compelling way.

Married to her beloved Sarath for over sixty years, they spent the majority of their married life in the UK, and made many friends, while maintaining close ties with their relatives and childhood friends back home. Hers is, therefore, a life lived in two cultures, having to adapt to life in a foreign country, and coming to love and be loved by many here, but always aware of her roots elsewhere.

Family life has not always been straightforward with a number of significant challenges to face, but time after time, Norma has found God to be a faithful Father who watches over His children and responds as only the Father can to the cries of His own. This is a book that tells of the miraculous interventions of God in the life of a faithful and godly family. Reading it will build your faith in an all-powerful God and develop your love for His beloved Son.

—John Ellwood

Author, Pastor & Former Head Teacher

INTRODUCTION

My name is Norma, and I am married to Sarath Alahendra. We have three sons, who are all married, and three grandchildren.

I was brought up in a loving family with good Christian values, and the Word of God was central to our upbringing. As a family, we always observed Sundays as the Sabbath day consecrated unto God, and at the age of eleven, I was confirmed into the Anglican church. The vicar told each of us to expect the Holy Spirit to come into us when the bishop laid hands on us. No sooner than he had laid hands on me, I experienced the joy of the Holy Spirit, and from that day on, I have had a wonderful closeness with Father God.

Having lived a long life, I was led by the Holy Spirit to write this book of my testimonies.

God is the same yesterday, today and forever.

Chapter 1

THE BEGINNING

There would be no book written by me, about the Father heart of God, had Sarath and I not met and married.

Sarath grew up in a Buddhist household. He lived with his mum and sister in Colombo, the capital of Sri Lanka, and His dad worked in a rubber plantation in the centre of the country. Sadly, Sarath became ill with typhoid when he was a little over one year old. Typhoid fever was considered fatal in those days. I am told that his mother, who was only twenty-nine years of age at the time, cried out to God to save her child and let her die instead, and that is what happened. Both Sarath's mother and the maid died of typhoid, leaving Sarath's dad with two little ones under the age of three.

Sarath and his sister ended up in a convent, where the nuns took care of the children during term time. The stories that Sarath tells me are heart breaking. He talks about his loneliness and being devoid of a mother's love, but, even then, God Almighty had His hand upon him and his sister. No doubt, the

Nuns took great care of them and prayed for them daily, and they both grew up well and received a good education.

Sarath found employment in a leading bank in Sri Lanka and God's favour was upon him. At the age of twenty-one, he was offered a placement in the London branch of the same bank. In 1954, he agreed to a transfer for five years, and once again, he left his familiar surroundings and travelled alone to London. God had His hand upon Sarath although he did not know it; the Holy Spirit was guiding him all the time.

In London, Sarath teamed up with a few other young men and began sharing a flat. One of these young men, Anselm, invited Sarath to a Billy Graham crusade, in 1956, at Wembley Stadium. Sarath does not remember the details but recollects that he went up for the altar call and invited Jesus to come into his life. He does not remember much but God does! God remembers and was with him from that very day until now. As you read on, you will see God's faithfulness. We may take this commitment lightly, but God clings on to us, closer than a brother. He sends us to the earth for a purpose and takes care of everything.

Sarath left London in September 1959 and continued working for the same bank in Sri Lanka. Anselm had returned earlier, and they met up once again in Sri Lanka. By that time, Anselm had been introduced to my older sister and they were engaged to be married.

I was growing up in Sri Lanka attending Methodist College which was a leading Christian school. I was nineteen years of age and already the Lord was proving to be a wonderful organiser and planner. He knows and grooms His children for the task He has planned for us.

My parents were God-fearing children of God. They loved the Lord, and God's favour was upon them. They were blessed abundantly. The favour of God was flowing in our lives. We, the children, were provided for, we lacked nothing, and the Word of God was central in our lives.

It was November 1959, the telephone rang, and there was a stranger on the phone wanting to speak to my dad. It transpired that Anselm, together with three of his friends, had been travelling down south to enjoy a long weekend at a tourist resort which was also a place of worship for the Buddhist and Hindus. This was about 150 miles away from Colombo, and they had organised it as a pleasure trip for the long weekend. Unfortunately, while they were happily driving along, a little girl ran across the road, and she was knocked down by their car and she would not survive. Anselm was the driver.

My dad was a leading lawyer in the country and straightaway decided to travel about fifty miles down to be with these young men and offer any assistance he could give them. Dad invited the four friends to come back with him to our home where they could discuss the case further. We could see my future brother-in-law was completely traumatised, totally shaken. Then, out of the corner of my eye, I had my first encounter with my future husband. God used this situation to bring about His plan and His purposes. Due to this accident, my dad met with these four friends regularly as he represented them as their lawyer. The case went on, and, in the meantime, plans for my sister's wedding to Anslem were moving along as well. The wedding was set for April 23rd, 1960.

Sarath and I were getting to know each other as friends; I was twenty and he was twenty-nine. In my mind it could be nothing more than a friendship. The day of my sister's wedding arrived. I was one of four bridesmaids and Sarath was one of four groomsmen. It was a grand occasion with over five hundred guests.

Towards the end of the wedding, to my complete surprise, Sarath asked me to marry him. I know I was shocked, but what shocked me more was that I accepted his proposal. Here was a man I hardly knew. Not only did I not know anything about him, and the age difference seem to be too great, but I was also hoping to go to medical school, should I get the required grades at the entrance examination. But more important than all these things, this person, whose proposal I had just accepted, was a Buddhist! *"Lord!"* I cried. *"Help! What should I do? My parents will never give their consent... I will be unequally yoked... God, will You bless this union?"*

The happiest night of my life turned out to be one of the saddest. I was afraid of my dad. What would he say? I was very tired but spent most of the night on my knees and in tears. Sarath left, saying he would not see me again till he had written to my dad and acquired his permission, which was the gentlemanly thing to do. As I had expected, Dad said no, and there began the most traumatic, awful year of my life. Yet somehow, I knew that God was faithful. He would give me the grace to face and to go through whatever the future held.

From that time, I was not allowed to leave the house without a chaperone. The telephone was locked, and Sarath and I had no contact with each other during that period. Sarath visited my dad in his office, during their lunch break, hoping to make my dad change his mind, but the answer was always the same. My parents used a lot of pressure, and then threats, to try to make me change my mind. I was so alone and helpless but spent a lot of time with Jesus. I would ask, *"What is Your will, Lord?"*

From what I could see, to go ahead with the marriage would've been against the will of God which clearly states, *"Do not be unequally yoked"* (2 Corinthians 6:14), but the Lord was my comforter. He never let go of me, always holding me in His everlasting arms. I knew that He was telling me that I had His approval, but how could it be so? He kept on reassuring me, that He was with me. How could I get my own parents to know this? When I told them that Jesus approved, they laughed at me saying, "That's very convenient isn't it?" It was a time of great anguish and mental and spiritual torment. But God was moving things around to reach Sarath.

My parents told me that, should I go against their wishes, they would cut me off from the family. They prophesied that the marriage would not last more than six months, but to the glory of God, it lasted sixty years! What a wonderful Father. But these words were so harsh to a twenty-year-old girl. The Lord kept on reassuring me that this was His plan and that I was in His will. God's eyes were on Sarath while He kept on strengthening me with His Grace. But why was this happening? How could this be happening?

The Father heart of God was taking care of Sarath. He did not forget Sarath's invitation for Him to come in and be his Lord back in 1956. By the time of Sarath's proposal, in 1960, God had gotten me ready. He had built up my faith and filled me with His grace, so that I could stand the onslaught of the enemy. He had prepared me to hear His voice, and obey Him by doing the unthinkable, by leaving home to marry this man.

It took Sarath thirty-three more years to admit to himself, to the Lord and the people around him (including me), that he had opened his heart to Jesus that night in 1956. God is alive, He hears us,

He knows us, He knows our going out and our coming in. He is abounding in grace and mercy. He will not let go of His children. Though our sins are as scarlet, He washes us whiter than snow and keeps us so close to Him. He is faithful, He is the Rock. He is the Anchor to our soul. Hallelujah!

Chapter 2

PEOPLE I MET BY DIVINE APPOINTMENT

SISTER AGNES 1969

Life was very difficult. I was unable to cope as our eldest son had special needs (I share more on this in chapter 5). His younger brothers were progressing very well in school while he was struggling to cope in a normal school whose teachers were not trained in teaching children with special needs. I too found it very hard to cope with. Most of my days were spent crying out to God for help. On one such afternoon, I had my head in my hands, having no one to seek help from, when there was a knock on the door. I was not expecting anyone but went to the door with three little children hanging on to me. There, standing at my front door, was this stranger dressed in white with a broad smile on her face. I did not know her; I had never met her before.

"Do not be afraid," she said. "God came to me in a dream last night. He showed me your home, where you live, and sent me to comfort you. You are loved.

He knows you. You are a chosen vessel. He is pleased with you. He knows you are troubled wondering if you have displeased the Lord, but He has sent me to reassure you that He loves you and is well pleased with you."

The more she went on, the more afraid I became, and the more she reassured me. Having grown up in the Anglican church, I was not familiar with the baptism of the Holy Spirit or the gifts of the Holy Spirit. I was afraid. I loved Jesus, I knew He died for me, but I did not understand what was happening. *Who was this person? Was she genuine?* She was reading my mind. She kept telling me not to be afraid. All this was happening at my front door. She said that she had walked about 5 miles under the guidance of the Holy Spirit and found me. After what seemed like a long time, she asked me if she could come in, all the time assuring me not to be afraid. I have come to tell you that Jesus loves you, He knows you, He is well pleased with you. You are chosen, your husband is chosen, your three children are chosen vessels. Your son whom the devil tried to steal and kill will be taken care of by God. *How did she know all this? How did this person, who I had never met before, know me?* But I invited her in, all the while wondering if I was making the right decision.

Having come in, she gave me her testimony. She was a young mother of two children worshipping in a Methodist church. At the age of twenty-nine she went totally blind. She sought help from the best of doctors but received no help from them and remained blind for about five years. She told me that she even had maggots coming out of her eyes! Her church had prayed for her, but she had still not received healing. She was completely alone trying to care for two little children and her husband. Her husband was a carpenter and was bringing a small income home. This was in the 1940 when there was no income support or benefits system in place.

One day, a nun from the local Pentecostal church visited her and informed her that an American healing evangelist was holding some healing meetings in their church and invited her to attend the meeting to which she readily agreed to go. She told me that no sooner than the pastor laid hands on her eyes she was "slain in the Spirit" (i.e., she fell to the ground by the power of God). These people understood what was happening, but she did not. She told me that she saw ladders coming down from Heaven and angels travelling down from Heaven and ministering to the people on Earth. She said that she had a glimpse of Heaven. She was later told that she was slain in the Spirit for quite a while.

When she awoke from her spiritual encounter, she was given a Bible to read, and to everyone's surprise, she was able to see perfectly! Sister Agnes had encountered God's presence, received the baptism of the Holy Spirit, and she had been anointed to preach the Gospel and lay hands on the sick. Her healing was complete.

However, when she got back home and stood in front of the mirror to look at her eyes, she was nauseated. The pupils of her eyes were just blobs of yellow. She cried out to God to remove the scars, "I am just twenty-nine years of age, please take these scars away, Lord!" Then God said, *"But if I take them away, no one will believe your testimony. This will be your story, but I will be with you always. Do not be ashamed."*

I was privileged to meet her and be friends with her for many years to come. The Lord knows us by name. I was beginning to understand the love of God. He watches over us. He loves us. He will move His people around to minister to us and to advance His Kingdom. I was meeting up with a woman of God, chosen and ordained by God, by divine appointment. She was operating in the gifts of the Holy Spirit. What an awesome God we serve! He is majestic. He knows each one of us. He knows our every thought. Though our sins are as scarlet He washes us whiter than snow. He puts His robe of righteousness over our sin-scarred bodies. He is slow to anger, abounding in grace. He is the great I AM. He is ALPHA and OMEGA. THE WAY, THE TRUTH, and THE LIFE. My redeemer, my friend. HALLELUIAH!

I had been walking around with so much guilt and shame. I had left home without my parents' consent, saying that I had heard from God. *But had I actually heard God? Was it just my own imagination for my own convenience?* The enemy was having a wonderful time accusing me, when actually, I was obeying the Lord. God knew the facts. Sarath had invited Jesus into His heart long before I came into his life. God was holding on to His child even though Sarath had pushed this thought to the back of his mind. He is faithful. When He said, *"I will never leave you nor forsake you[1]"*, He meant it. He will use His children to reach those He loves.

———————————————

[1] Hebrews 13:5

MY NEXT ENCOUNTER BY DIVINE APPOINTMENT

February 16th, 1973, was a new chapter in our lives. By the leading of the Holy Spirit, Sarath sadly gave up his job, we packed our belongings, sold our palatial home with everything that we had acquired, and embarked on a new journey. The company that Sarath worked for was a British company in Sri Lanka, and they transferred him to the head office in London for eighteen months to help us decide what we wanted to do regarding our future. This had to be God ordained; they knew our situation regarding our son and were very sympathetic. Again, it was God working, He was involved in every detail. The company expected us to work things out for ourselves in the eighteen months.

From now on, it was only God and us. We were living under a semi-communist government in Sri Lanka at the time, and they would not let citizens leave the country with any foreign currency. We were allowed just £5 pocket money for the journey, so we left trusting God to take care of our every need.

We arrived at Heathrow Airport on a cold winter's morning. Sarath and I were scared but the three boys were excited. A kind friend met us and took us to a one bed apartment in Finchley, North London. The apartment belonged to his friend who had generously let us, total strangers, occupy her home for the duration of her ten-day vacation. It was wonderful to know that we had a roof over our heads for at least ten days. God was using unbelievers to help us at the point of our need. What a God! We had to learn to trust Him for all our needs from then on.

Sarath started work in his new job at a much lower position than what he had back home. It must have been so hard for him. In Sri Lanka, he was a big fish in a small pond, but now he was a small fish in a large pond. God was asking him to sacrifice his career for the sake of his family and I had to watch him make that sacrifice. It was not easy, but somehow God sustained him and us. The Lord was able to bring us through this period because Sarath said yes to Him.

I can imagine what Abraham must have felt like when the Lord asked him to leave everything behind: his family, his friends, his comfort zone, and move to live in a tent (Genesis 12:1). Sarath had the additional burden of finding a place for us to live in ten days' time. Our three boys were nine, ten, and twelve years old. Every letting agent he went to said that landlords would not accept tenants who were non-English or with children. But, once again, the Lord's favour was upon us and Sarath was offered a house in Northolt in Middlesex. Not a place we were familiar with but somehow God was moving us along, according to His plans and purposes.

My knowledge of the Father heart of God at that time was not what it is now but this much I knew: God is a good God. He is so big! He is a big, BIG God. He is alive. He will never leave us. He was holding the five of us in the palm of His hand, guiding us beside still waters, leading us to green pastures and preparing a table for us daily. We never went hungry, nor did we run out of provisions. He had shown us throughout our son's illness that all He asked of us was to trust Him. We were five of His children moving in obedience to His leading.

Isaiah 43:1-3 says:

> *"But now, thus says the Lord, who created you, O Jacob, And He who formed you, O Israel: Fear not, for I have redeemed you; I have called you by your name; You are Mine. When you pass through the waters, I will be with you; And through the rivers, they shall not*

overflow you. When you walk through the fire, you shall not be burned, Nor shall the flame scorch you. For I am the Lord your God, The Holy One of Israel, your Savior..."

Every situation that came up, He was there with us. Such strength, such comfort to know that the Most High God was our Father, taking care of every situation.

Even the children's schooling was taken care of. We would have loved to send the two younger boys to private schools but that was not in God's plan. He made sure that nothing of this world would hinder our walk with Him. We had to learn to live a Kingdom lifestyle, and the things of this world had to be left behind while we learnt to seek first the Kingdom of God.

Our new landlord was a very exacting Sikh man who insisted on keeping a key to the house. He realised that we went to church every Sunday and decided to spend Sundays in the house on the pretext of doing maintenance work. We often came back home from church to find his family occupying the sitting room and garden; nevertheless, God was using this to teach us humility. We were at this man's mercy; he knew our plight and decided to exploit the situation.

Every six months, he would telephone, increasing the rent once again, and exploiting the predicament we were in. We had three children, and he was aware that it was not easy for us to find rented accommodation. I have no idea how we got through that period of our lives, but the Lord was our strength. It was His hand on us that got us through.

Our three boys, who were used to all the luxuries of life, were now having to adapt to a life of poverty. Even now my heart breaks when I think of the times that I had to say "no" to an ice cream cone because I could not afford the 10p. The van would often park outside our house, knowing that there were three children indoors. The thing I remember most was how good the boys were. When I explained to them that I could not afford it, they would simply carry on playing without complaining.

The Lord opened doors for us to admit Dilip, our eldest, to a school for children with special needs just half a mile from our home. Once more, His hand was upon us. Now we could understand why the Lord had secured this home for us; He sees to everything. He is the ever-seeing, ever-knowing God. We were called up for an interview by the headmaster who was a very compassionate, understanding man. Unfortunately, he told us that we had arrived at the school too late, as Dilip was twelve years old, and they would teach him basic things like managing money and crossing the road (but God had a different plan).

During this period of our lives, I found it very hard. I felt alone, abandoned, and even wondered if we had really heard from the Holy Spirit in our move to the UK. But I must say that I always knew God was with us. Doubts do come at times like this, but He strengthened us, taught us, revealed Himself to us, and He was very gentle with us.

One afternoon I had my head in my hands, crying out to God from my innermost being, when I heard a letter being delivered through the letter box. *Who could this be?* No one knew where we lived. *Who would write to us?* I was full of self-pity, a time when my focus was on myself rather than upwards unto God. But God was teaching me His ways. He was teaching me to put my focus on Him rather than on my circumstances. As I picked up the letter, I saw that it was addressed to me and posted from Tulsa Oklahoma, USA. *Who could this be from?* I did not know anyone in Tulsa. As I opened the letter, I discovered that the sender's name was ORAL

ROBERTS. I had no idea who he was, nor how he came to know my name, nor where I lived.

It transpired that he was a leading evangelist who was writing to me to say that God loved me, God had chosen me, and God knew my name. *How could this happen?* It was obvious that someone had passed on my name to him, but up to this day, I still do not know who. Oral Roberts told me that God knew what difficulties we were facing, and that He wanted to help me by revealing His love for us. By now I was trembling with excitement, my heart was racing. *How did Oral Roberts know how to reach me?* So similar to the way that Sister Agnes, in Sri Lanka, had found us. *Lord, is this really You? Is this actually happening to me?*

I felt led to reply to the letter, and from then on began a correspondence between Oral Roberts and I that lasted for over twenty years. He was my mentor who taught me so much about the love, compassion, joy, grace, and peace of God. Oral Roberts was a prolific writer and he sent me all of his books free of charge, and I was privileged to learn SO MUCH about my Lord and Saviour.

Oral was a man of faith. God healed him and raised him from his death bed and anointed him to heal the sick at the age of seventeen. He was used by God to build a university completely debt free and to educate the whole man. He taught me to plant a seed and to expect it to multiply and produce a harvest. He taught me that God was a good God, a God of multiplication who wanted His children to prosper and be in good health even as our souls prosper. I learnt that God was my source of total supply. He was the all-sufficient God, and my sufficiency is in Him.

My husband and I were privileged to travel to Tulsa on two occasions to meet Brother Oral. He taught us that God was a miracle working God, He taught us about tithing out of gratitude and not out of compulsion.

On one occasion, Sarath came home from work saying that we had to go back to Sri Lanka once his contract at work was over because his pension would not be sufficient for us to live on. I was heartbroken as this meant we would have to leave our children behind in the UK, as they would all be adults by then. It is easy for a child to venture out leaving parents behind, which is what we did, in 1973, but it is not so easy for a parent to leave their children behind. This was going to be hard. As usual, we went to the Lord and asked Him what we should do.

While I was seeking God, I heard him say, *"Will you trust Me with all you have?"* He led me to Luke 6:38:

> *'Give, and it will be given to you: good measure, pressed down, shaken together, and running over will be put into your bosom. For with the same measure that you use, it will be measured back to you.' (Luke 6:38)*

The Lord showed me that we only have to give once, and He will give back seven times over. In God's economy, seven means *complete*. This means His reward for our trust in Him is seven times over; His reward for our trust in Him is complete.

"Give, and:
1. *It shall be:*
2. *Given unto you,*
3. *Good measure,*
4. *Pressed down,*
5. *Shaken together,*
6. *Running over…*
7. *Into your bosom."*

I wanted no unbelief in what I was about to do, so I decided not to tell anyone. I decided to plant my seed into a project that Brother Oral had begun, which I believed was good soil. He was building a university through which the Lord had directed him to "educate the whole man". So, when I received my salary that month, I planted the entire amount into that project, as a seed, expecting God to multiply it. Normally, my income was used for housekeeping, so it was easy not to let others know what I was doing. Thank God, no one knew, and the Lord enabled me to feed us all for that month, without any hardship. The larder ran dry, the freezer was emptied, but the Lord sustained us and fed us. As long as I kept my focus upwards, I did not waver.

After about three months, Sarath came home full of smiles. "You will never guess what happened today," he said. The company Sarath worked for had announced a very generous "share option scheme", which would give employees shares in the company at a discounted price in proportion to their current salary. This went on for a few years, and each time they received a pay rise or increment, they were allotted more shares. Then as suddenly as it came, it was also stopped; nevertheless, by now we had more than enough to sustain us for the rest of our lives in the UK — isn't God amazing! Wonderful! Awesome!

God said that He would bless us to be a blessing (Genesis 12:2), and that is exactly what He did. As

He blessed us, we were able to be a blessing to others as well. Even the rest of the employees in that company were being blessed because a child of God was amongst them. God said that He would give "...*good measure, pressed down, shaken together, and running over...*" and that is what He did! Thirty years on from that day, we are still reaping the fruit of that harvest. The Lord God is sovereign; what He said, He did. It happened. He is Truth. He never lies, His word does not return to Him void; He can be trusted. Praise God!

Chapter 3

THE HEALING POWER OF GOD

JON

A young boy named Jon, the son of a friend of ours, went on holiday to Spain with his family. While there, he fell ill with a collapsed lung and was unable to fly back. Our friend, Jon's mum, was a general practitioner (GP) and extended their stay to take care of Jon until he was well enough to travel. In the meantime, Jon's dad and sister decided to fly back home.

A short while later, we were attending our home group Bible study, at their home, when Jon's mum took me upstairs and asked me to pray for Jon's complete healing. By this time, they had returned home from Spain.

Matthew 10:8 says:

> *"Heal the sick, cleanse the lepers, raise the dead, cast out demons. Freely you have received, freely give."*

Jesus commanded us to lay hands on the sick in His name. My immediate reaction was panic but then I realised that I could do nothing of myself, but in Christ — the Christ who lives in me — I could perform or do anything because He is a miracle working God.

I prayed silently, *"Jesus have mercy on us. Use my hands and heal Jon."* Then I laid hands on his chest, commanded the spirit of infirmity to leave Jon's body, and then gave thanks for the healing that was taking place.

Jon testified that he felt the power of God surge through his body and he has had no problems with his lungs since that day. Today he is a doctor, serving God by healing others. God loves all. He watches over His children and uses anyone who is willing to be used by Him.

> *"You are the light of the world. A city that is set on a hill cannot be hidden."* (Matthew 5:14)

These are words spoken by Jesus and we are called to obey His Word. His Word is sovereign and does not return to Him void.

IAN

It was a cold December evening. The Council had granted the churches in Harrow permission to sing Christmas carols in the shopping mall. After closing time (6 pm), we all assembled in the mall, took our places, and began to sing carols led by a symphony orchestra whose conductor was Ian, a member of one of the other churches. It was a glorious occasion. I am sure the angels of the Kingdom of Heaven were there with us, as we produced such beautiful music which did surely glorify the Lord. There were many faiths present in the audience who seem to be truly touched by the presence of God.

Two days later, my friend from church, who is a GP, telephoned me asking if we were free the next afternoon. I told her we were, and she informed us that Ian, the conductor of the orchestra, had suffered a stroke and was in hospital. The doctors could not understand what had caused it, he was only in his forties but was now unable to stand or move as he was completely paralysed. She asked if we could join her at 3pm at the hospital to pray for Ian. She also told us that she had called the vicar, the leadership, and some others from the healing team to pray for him but none of them were available. It was only after that, that she thought of calling us. Straight away my flesh rose up in pride: *We are only thought of when the important people are not available, we are simply an afterthought...* This is how the enemy operates. He kept taunting us, saying, "You are going to make a fool of yourself, who do you think you are?"

Nevertheless, we knew that these thoughts were not of God. The Lord knew He could use us. So, we had to repent. Then we went into a time of deep prayer. Genuine, heartfelt prayer full of remorse and repentance. *"Lord, if you can use us, please use us, but as for me I am terribly frightened."* He then reminded me that we do not have to do anything ourselves but that it was His responsibility. I do not think I slept all night. *"Is anything too hard for the Lord? I am only a vessel that will be a conduit for Him. Lord, glorify Your name. I love You and I'm grateful that You want to use us."*

We woke up to a cold wintry morning; I looked out and saw a blanket of snow. Both Sarath and I were experiencing all the symptoms of the flu and looking for any excuse not to go. But we were determined not to be governed by our feelings, instead to go to the hospital just focused on the Lord and only the Lord.

We met our friend, who took us to the patient, and we spent some time reading the Scriptures with him, getting his focus away from himself up onto Jesus. We wheeled him to the hospital chapel, and I asked him if we could pray for him. When he said yes, we reminded him of the miracles that Jesus did. We said, "The same Jesus who healed those people in the Gospels is now with us. He is the same yesterday today and forever. If we ask Him and believe that He is the same Jesus, He will heal you, Ian. He is full of compassion and mercy."

First, God led us to pray for Ian's salvation. We asked the Lord to reveal Himself to Ian and to fill him with the Holy Spirit. To our surprise, Ian, who had been so quiet up to that point began to shout, "Please don't stop! This is so wonderful, so amazing, I feel awesome!" My husband and I immediately laid hands on him and said, "Ian, be healed in Jesus' name." We were privileged to watch the Lord at work. We recognised the work of the Lord happening before our very eyes. We had nothing to do with this. Jesus did not ask His disciples to pray for the sick but lay hands on the sick, and that is what we did. Unfortunately for us, there were no visible signs of healing. He did not jump out of his chair, he just sat on it and smiled at us. We left him in the chapel with his wife and went home.

The next day, our friend telephoned to say that Ian was discharged. Apparently, the nurses found him out of his chair, walking, packed and ready to go home. I asked Jesus what had happened, and Jesus said that if Ian had jumped out of his wheelchair in the chapel the focus and the glory would have been on us, but now the glory goes only to Jesus. Our God is awesome, glorious, abounding in grace and mercy. Our God is faithful. He answered our childlike faith. All the while training us to minister in His name and to trust Him to do the work.

PARA

Para was a very dear, close family friend of ours. He was Chief Executive of one of Sri Lanka's leading banks, and a religious man, who revered and respected god. Unfortunately, he was not a Christian. He had a beautiful wife and two married daughters who were devout Hindus and kept all feasts and traditions of their faith. He had arrived in the UK for a cataract operation at Moorfields Eye Hospital because the operation done in Sri Lanka, for one eye, was not successful and he was left totally blind in that eye.

We visited them at their daughter's home on the evening before the operation. Although they were Hindus, I plucked up the courage to ask him if we could pray for him to Jesus, because we could see and sense the fear in him. After we prayed, he said that the fear lifted, and he felt so peaceful. He faced the operation the next morning and was discharged the same day. Nothing spectacular happened, but Para and his wife reported that the operation was a success and that he now had perfect vision in that eye. He said that there was no more fear of blindness because God had answered our prayers.

They returned to Sri Lanka and, to our surprise, went about proclaiming the goodness of Jesus to everyone they knew, including our sisters. They testified that Jesus had healed Para and prevented him from going blind. To God be the glory! Two Hindus evangelising about the goodness of Jesus! I can picture Jesus in the throne room of God with all the angels, dancing, and rejoicing. What a scene that must have been.

After some years had passed, we had a telephone call from Para, this time from Australia. They were visiting his daughter and family in Sydney. They told us that they were getting ready to go back to

Sri Lanka, but before the return journey they thought it would be a good idea to have a full medical check-up in Australia. Unfortunately, what was just a medical check-up turned out to be bad news, in fact, a nightmare.

This is how Para broke the news to us: "Norma, do you remember praying for me in the UK the night before my cataract operation?"

"Yes," I replied.

"Well, something happened to me that day... Now I have been told that I have late-stage cancer of my hip... I am not fit for travelling. I am in severe pain... but I know that if you pray for me, I should feel better."

I told him I would certainly pray. I told him that God loved him so much and did not want him to suffer. "God can and will perform miracles and God has a plan for each one of us," I said. "God knows your heart, Para."

I told him that God sees and has seen his faithfulness. I then explained the gospel as best as I could over the telephone. I explained the power in the name of Jesus, and I asked him to use that name every time the pain came on. That is what they did, each time the pain came on they called on Jesus and sometimes telephoned us for comfort.

We would lead them in prayer, always explaining the love of Jesus, trying our best to get the focus on Almighty God, our Saviour, our Healer, and our Deliverer. It was not easy to minister to someone so far away, but God made the way for us to do so. We too were learning that there was no distance in prayer. God is the all-encompassing Lord.

In the meantime, I telephoned Jesse Duplantis Ministries, in the UK, and spoke to them about our friend in Australia. I told them our friend was ripe for harvest and asked if they could send someone from their office in Australia to minister to our friend. Thank the Lord they did. They would minister to our friend along with us. Isn't the Lord wonderful? Our friend, who was in Australia, contacted us in the UK, and we contacted Jesse Duplantis Ministries who arranged for someone to visit and counsel our friend in Sydney, and then introduce them to the Hillsong church.

This is how important each one of us is to the Lord. He will move His people around the globe to help His children. Such a faithful God! Nothing is too hard for Him, each one of us is precious in His sight. After all, God Almighty allowed His Son, Jesus, to sacrifice His life, to deliver us from the kingdom of darkness and place us in the Kingdom of God. We counselled Para about death and the life beyond, and the way to the Kingdom of God. Being a practising Hindu, he believed in many gods, so to add Jesus to the list of gods was not hard for him. We had to convince him that there was only one God, and His name is Jesus. He is alive!

We cried out to the Lord, *"Father You know Para, that he is a praying man, faithful and God-fearing. He now needs Your help. He acknowledges that You are the healer, please, Lord, reveal Yourself to him. Prove to him that you are the only true God. I do not know how you can do it, but You are God, and nothing is impossible for You. Please do not let him leave this earth without an encounter with You."* I thought of the story about Cornelius being a God-fearing man.

After some time, Para began to feel better and was given permission to travel back home to Sri Lanka. It was a miracle that he made the fourteen-hour journey. Nevertheless, he did it and we continued keeping in touch and praying for him.

What an awesome, miracle working God we serve! God performed the impossible. Our friend's wife told us that one afternoon, as they were resting, she heard him call out for her loudly. She ran to enquire what it was and saw that he was seated on the bed saying, "Jesus is in the room". She thought he was hallucinating because she could see nothing. However, the Lord had opened his spiritual eyes to see Him although his wife could not. When he kept insisting that Jesus was in the room with arms wide open saying, "I have come to take you home", she told Para that he must tell Jesus that he cannot come.

"I have to go. Jesus is calling," he replied.

"You can't go," she said. "What is going to happen to me? I can't live alone; you have always taken care of me. Tell Jesus you can't come."

These two were married for over 50 years. If it were possible to have a perfect marriage, they had one. However, Para insisted that he had to go, and he was certain Jesus would take care of her.

God knows each one of us, He loves us unconditionally. What awesome love! We come to this world alone, and we leave it alone. God makes sure that He is there to receive us. We are never alone; the only criterion is that we believe His word. There is nothing that we need to do. His grace is sufficient in our weakness. What amazing, awesome love! Jesus gave His life so that no one may perish if they believe in Him. If we come to Him, acknowledge Him as Saviour, that He died and rose again to pay the penalty for our sin, He washes these sin-stained bodies with His precious blood, clothes us with His robe of righteousness and takes us home to spend eternity with Him. Eternal life is a reality.

We each make the choice as to where we spend eternity. When we acknowledge Jesus, we are translated from the kingdom of darkness into the kingdom of light, which is where Almighty God is. The love of God for each one of us is beyond understanding, but so true. Jesus is the only way to the Father, He is the gateway, the door. The Scriptures say pray that you may know how wide, how broad, how high, how deep the Father's love for you is. Pray daily for the revelation of God's love for us and He will open our eyes to the magnitude of His incomparable love. Such love!

Well, Para went home to be with the Lord. Sri Lankan funerals are attended by large crowds, and Para's wife told the people, "My husband did not die of cancer. Cancer could not have him; Jesus came and took him home." What a testimony! To God be the glory, people were amazed at what they were hearing. God will always have His way; He used this couple for His glory. Hallelujah!

GALL BLADDER

My husband Sarath was experiencing abdominal pains and was referred to a hospital clinic for investigation. A scan revealed a group of stones which the consultant radiologist likened to a bunch of grapes. Sarath was then scheduled for surgery in a fortnight's time.

On admission, the surgeon said that he needed to have a second look at the scan for himself. In the meantime, we, the family, and some friends, had prayed and asked the Lord Jesus Christ to heal Sarath. The Word of God says that we can command the stones to dissolve and pass out of his body, and that is what we dared to believe. We spoke to the stones in the name of Jesus Christ and ordered them to move.

The surgeon was looking at the two scans and was looking quite puzzled. "Sarath, I'm very sorry, but I cannot see any stones. Do you mind if I consult your original radiologist at her new hospital?" It took a while for the original radiologist to come over but the two of them had a consultation. Afterwards, they came over to Sarath's bed apologising for the inconvenience they had caused him and showed him the two scans saying, "They are completely different. In one scan there were very clearly a group of stones but in the other scan there are no sign of stones!"

We understood what had happened. Our wonderful Jesus had performed an amazing miracle. He is ALIVE! He is God! He is THE TRUTH. He never lies. He hears us when we pray to Him in the name of Jesus.

His Word says:

> "...I have heard your prayer, I have seen your tears; surely I will heal you." (2 Kings 20:5)

What an awesome God He is! Such is the Father heart of my God. Sarath was discharged from the hospital that evening. His gall bladder has not troubled him since, and He still keeps the letter of apology given by the hospital for the inconvenience caused.

GLAUCOMA

About the same time, Sarath went for a routine eye test. The optometrist suspected glaucoma and referred him to the eye hospital.

We noticed that the Lord always gave us time between appointments. He was training us to get our focus on Him whatever the condition. The Lord is our Healer, our Deliverer.

The appointment was given for two months later. As expected, there was no glaucoma, and we were discharged with a good report. That was forty years ago and still no glaucoma! Praise God! We give Him all the glory and the honour.

THE MERCY OF GOD

We attended a routine appointment at the GP surgery at 11am. Sarath was prescribed some antibiotics because the GP felt that his lungs were not clear. After we got back home, Sarath complained of feeling extremely tired and wanted to go to bed. He was very restless and kept on saying that he could not express what he felt but that he feels something is very wrong. He came back to the sitting room complaining that he was feeling warm and sweaty. I gave him the GTN spray and was observing him, wondering what I should do.

The time now was about 3.30pm. Sarath asked me to help him get to bed, so I got up from my chair and tried to help him up when suddenly he fell back in the chair. I noticed that he was sweating profusely, it was as though somebody had poured a bucket of water over him. The next moment, his head went back, and he was gurgling.

I spoke to him but there was no response. My first instinct was to ring for the ambulance, but somehow my mind was completely blank. I could not remember a simple number like 999. I could not even remember our children's telephone numbers. In hindsight, I can see God's hand in all this, but I could not see it then.

The next thing I remember was me, with both my hands on Sarath's chest, screaming out the name of Jesus! There is no other name that has power like the name of Jesus. When we are in the middle of the storm He is there. When we are in the raging waters, He is there. As we go through the fire, He says we will not burn. That is our Lord. So faithful, so true, so compassionate, full of grace, abounding in mercy. His Word is TRUTH.

We were in that storm but not alone. Jesus was with me.

> *"Behold, the eye of the Lord is on those who fear Him, on those who hope in His mercy,"* *(Psalm 33:18)*

> *"The angel of the Lord encamps all around those who fear Him, and delivers them."*
> *(Psalm 34:7)*

Sarath came back after what seemed like eternity. But he came back with praise and worship on his lips. He says he cannot recollect any of this, but we, the family, know that the Lord touched him in a very profound and powerful way. The glory of the Lord was shining on his face. He was so bright and full of light. There was no more darkness, only peace and joy. Praise God and glory to His name forever more. We truly serve a living God who is worthy to be praised. Amen and amen.

The next morning, we visited the surgery once more and were referred to the Royal Brompton Hospital in London. The prognosis was not good. Even before any tests were done, we were told that it looked like a blocked valve in his heart which needed surgery fairly urgently. He was said to have an Aortic Stenosis. The cardiologist spoke to us and said that there was only a 20% chance of recovery because he was very weak, and he already had six stents inserted. We had no choice but to let them do a procedure called a "TAVI" (Transcatheter aortic valve implantation).

The favour of God was upon us. We had a very compassionate cardiologist who knew what we were going through, and he even allowed us to stay outside the theatre and kept on sending us messages about the progress Sarath was making. At the end of the surgery, he popped his head out and gave us a thumbs up sign to indicate that it had gone well.

Sarath was in Harefield Hospital for ten days. He was given two blood transfusions during his stay and then ultimately discharged from hospital. We were quite nervous, but we knew that the Word of God says that even when we walk through the valley of the shadow of death, He is with us (Psalm 23). The Lord Jesus had sustained us. He never leaves us. The angels assigned to each one of us were encamped around us, guarding, and protecting us. We always felt His arms around us. What a God! What an amazing Father!

While Sarath was in hospital, I was led by the Holy Spirit to contact Kingdom Faith Bible School and inquire if Pastor Collin Urquhart would lay hands and pray for Sarath. Pastor Colin wanted to know how we knew of him, and I said that the two of us had been students at the college in 1993/94. He also asked what Sarath's condition was, to which I replied "very serious". The favour of God was once more on us when Pastor Collin asked if we could bring Sarath straight from the hospital to Horsham, even before we had got back home. This was a one-hundred-and-fifty-mile round trip, but the Lord did not allow fear to grip me. Instead, He lifted me above the fear and made faith arise. This was an instruction from the Lord, not from me. Our son and I made the decision to take Sarath who, under normal conditions, was not fit to do this journey, but we knew that these instructions came from the Lord.

Pastor Collin was so gracious and compassionate. He had arranged for us to be ministered to as close as possible to the entrance; just him and the three of us. We could sense the Father heart of God, with so much compassion. It was an amazing experience.

Thank You God for Your love. AMEN and AMEN!

Sarath made a full recovery.

Chapter 4

THE PRESENCE OF GOD

THE AROMA OF CHRIST

There were times in my life when the room would suddenly be filled with a sweet aroma. At times, I was quite baffled by this, but I gradually came to recognise it and called it the aroma of Christ. It was a mixture of sandalwood, incense, and the sweet-smelling fragrance of apples, pears, lavender, and roses. Sometimes it was just a fleeting scent, sometimes it was a lingering smell, but it was always a sweet and pleasant aroma.

As I began to recognise it, I used to talk to Him, *"Is that You, Lord?"* I would shut my eyes and bask in His presence. There were a few occasions when my husband recognised that fragrance too. What an honour. Almighty God, The Great I Am, coming to visit His children. This must have been what Adam and Eve experienced, when the Lord came down to visit them every evening.

TOUCH

There have been a few occasions, not many, when I have felt the touch of God on my shoulder. A time I remember vividly was at Wembley Arena; we were attending a Jesus conference. While waiting for the meeting to begin, I felt a great wind brush past me. As it travelled, He stopped by me, tapping my shoulder, and then moving along. To me, this was a sign of approval from Jesus, letting me know that He wanted us to be there.

Sometimes a gentle wind, sometimes a light wind, and yet at times a firm touch. Thank You Holy Spirit that You know me so well.

DREAMS

Very early in my walk with the Lord, I had a dream. I was attending a funeral with two graves. The coffins were being lowered into the graves and the bishop of Colombo, who was also my uncle, was conducting the funerals. As the coffins were being lowered, the lid of one of the coffins opened and the body came out of it. All the while the other burial carried on.

The body that came out was mine, while the other body was my mother's. I did not understand the significance of the dream at the time. However, I now know that these types of prophetic dreams are shown to us so that we can pray against them or for them.

I was eight months pregnant with my third child, and had the Lord not intervened, I could have bled to death on the delivery table. Thank God for Jesus, His hands were upon me. My son and I both survived this ordeal. He had a plan and a purpose for both our lives.

Unfortunately, my mother, who was only sixty-three years of age, went to be with the Lord three months later. The cause of death on her death certificate was a surgical misadventure. It is still too painful to recall it all, but I thank God that she was a believer. She was a wonderful woman of God who taught us, her children, what she knew about her Saviour.

Had I known then, what I know now, I wonder if I could have helped prolong her life through prayer? I do not know. But I know she was far too young to leave us. Why else did God show me that funeral? I do not know the full answer to that, but I am sure the Lord will reveal all one day (either on this side of eternity or the other).

MISSION TO LONDON

We attended the Mission to London conference hosted by Morris Cerullo in Earls Court for five days. We noticed that at every session (two a day) they would send an offertory bucket around asking the participants to put in their offerings. We found this difficult to accept. We felt there was too much pressure on us to keep on giving in this way. So, we decided to keep our wallets at home for one session. *Surely the Lord does not want His children to feel they have to give money when they do not have it?* All the while praying, *"Please forgive us if we are wrong to feel this way."*

As the meeting started, the evangelist preached on giving unto God and expecting to receive a one-hundred-fold harvest back from Him. I kept asking God to guide us in this venture. *"If these people are preaching the wrong message, please help us to discern."* But as the buckets were being passed, I told my husband that I really felt we should make an offering. I asked him if he had any money on him, but he didn't since we had decided not to bring any with us.

While the offering was being taken, the preacher said to turn to certain Scriptures. I took out my Bible, and, lo and behold, as I opened it, there was a $100 bill at that very page! Right there, in Earls Court, in the UK, God had provided me with one hundred American dollars for the offering!

Isn't God awesome! He is not a magician, but He knows our hearts. He knew I wanted to give, and He knew I was genuine. He satisfied my heart's desire. The Lord is the God of the harvest. To God be the glory, amen.

LOTTERY

Around this same time, the UK decided to introduce the national lottery.

There were so many discussions taking place. Would this encourage gambling in the country? Could people end up getting addicted to it? Is it correct for Christians to participate in this worldly pursuit? We are in the world, but not of this world... Would Jesus approve? So much confusion...

I decided to go to the Lord about this matter. *"Lord, what would You advise us, Your children, to do? We are being tested and tempted by this... Suppose we Christians do the lottery and win; wouldn't it be nice to use it to serve You, Lord? I have so many thoughts and questions, but it has to be Your will, Father."*

As was my custom, once the family left in the morning, I went for a walk about forty minutes around the block through the park. I was passing the post office when the question popped up again in my mind. *Should I walk in and purchase a ticket?* It was so new, and I did not know how to do the lottery. Again, the temptation was so great. "*Lord, should I go in? If I go in what are the numbers?*" I walked up to the door, turned back, ran out the door, and then went forward towards the door again. I did this three times. I ended up not buying the ticket that day, but I did have six numbers going around inside my head.

When Saturday arrived, and as the lottery was being drawn on TV, I kept calling out the numbers that God gave me before they were drawn. The Lord had heard me say that I would use the winnings to spread the gospel. He heard me, trusted me, and gave me the winning numbers but I did not believe that He would do it. He trusted me, but I did not believe Him.

I now know that when we pray and ask God for anything in faith, we must believe that He hears us and expect Him to answer the prayer.

Norma & Sarath, 1962,
18 months into marriage.

1967 Colombo — Norma, Sarath and their 3 sons Dilip (right),
Nihal (middle), Senaka (left)

Norma & Sarath with their granddaughter
Melina.

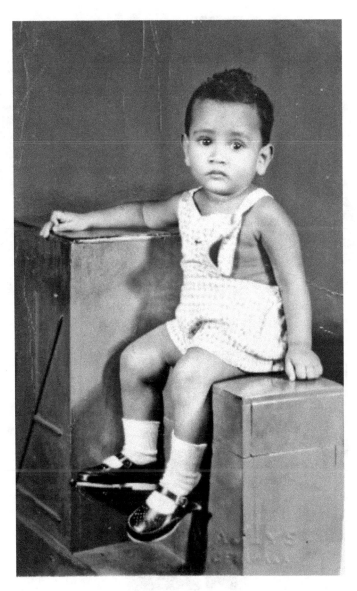

Dilip age 1 or 2

Dilip, in his Ministry of Defence
uniform, with Sarath (1986).

Sarath & his sister, 1933.

1968 visiting London for 6 months,
outside Buckingham Palace.

Family photo 2008.
Norma, Sarath, their 3 sons and their wives.

Norma, Sarath and 2 of their sons.

Norma and Sarath (1990).

Norma (1985)

Chapter 5

CELEBRATION OF A LIFE CREATED BY GOD FOR GOD

Dilip, our first born, came into the world on February 12th, 1962. He was wonderfully, perfectly, and fearfully made in the image of God. He was a beautiful little boy, a little bundle of joy, a little gift from God to us. As all parents know, a baby is so helpless and entirely dependent on its parents to make all decisions for him. We consulted the best paediatrician in Sri Lanka and was advised to immunise the baby.

After a few days, Dilip developed a fever, was listless, and not showing any interest in his surroundings. The fever was not responding to any medication. As young parents we did not know what to do. We consulted the GP daily, who was also my uncle, only to be told not to worry. Then on August 4th, 1962, our world was thrown into chaos. I went to the cot, to check on my baby, and found him unconscious! Our baby, who only a week earlier was sitting up and making gurgling baby sounds, was now lifeless, simply lying in his cot.

We rushed him to the doctor only to be told that there was nothing they could do, but we were advised to take the child to the hospital. It was now about 4pm, and Dilip was not seen by a consultant for around another two hours. When we did finally see a consultant, she spent about three hours with Dilip and came out of the room to tell us that he was seriously ill with Encephalitis.

In fact, her actual words were, "How old are you? You are so young, and you can have other children. Go home and prepare yourselves for the worst." To which I replied, "I serve a mighty God who loves us. He will not let Dilip die. This is my firstborn and I know that he will live." I did not know the Lord as I know Him now, but this much I knew: He honours faith. He loves us, and He can do the impossible.

Sarath was not with me when this doctor spoke these negative words to me because he had been sent to buy some scarce medicine. After he returned, we were asked to sign a consent form for a lumber puncture, which we signed. It pierced our hearts when we heard our baby, who had been unconscious, scream in pain; however, in hindsight, we know that it was good news, telling us that life was coming back into his lifeless body. The devil was trying his best to destroy Dilip, but

God had said, *"I am with you always. Do not be afraid, even though you walk through the valley of the shadow of death you will fear no evil."*

The next morning, the doctor came in to see Dilip. Seeing the Bible under his pillow, she asked me if I was a Christian, to which I said yes.

"I am a Buddhist," she said, "but I have to admit that your God worked a miracle last night. I did not expect this child to survive the night."

But the devil would not go down without a fight.

The next afternoon, Dilip was unconscious again with a fever; his temperature was 108 degrees Fahrenheit. The medical staff laid him in a tub of ice trying to get his temperature down. All Sarath and I could do was get down on our knees and call upon the Lord from the depths of our souls. I prayed, *"Lord, I am a young girl with nothing to offer You but my life. I give You my life and everything I am. I dedicate this child to You, use him for Your glory. As for me, I promise to shout from every mountain top about Your goodness and Your faithfulness."* And this is what I have done for the last sixty years.

Dilip clung to life with every fibre of his being. During this time many people came to tell us that the wrath of God was upon us. Again and again, we had to affirm that the God we serve is a God of love. Dilip was in hospital for a month and finally we were told we could take him home, but, just before we left the hospital, we were called in to the doctor's office with bad news once again. She said, "You two seem so happy to take your baby home, but I am wondering if we should have fought so hard to save his life. I have to warn you that this child will never walk or talk, he will be deaf, blind, and not have any teeth. In fact, he will not even get out of his bed." If ever there was a curse put on anyone, this was it. We did not know then what we know now, but the Holy Spirit caused me to rebuke this by saying, "My God performed a miracle that night, and you said so. When He does something, it is final. This child we are taking home will walk, will talk, will see, and hear." And under my breath I said, "Dilip will survive to serve the Lord." In fact, within a month of leaving the hospital, Dilip cut his first tooth, and he was able to lift his head once more. Praise God! Hallelujah!! Before long, he even began to crawl, and then walk. The only thing that was slow was his speech.

A few years later, in 1968, the Lord opened a door for us to travel to the UK, which gave us the opportunity to bring Dilip to Great Ormond Street Hospital in London. Having looked at all the reports from Sri Lanka, and done various tests and scans on Dilip, the doctors told us that there was nothing wrong with the child, absolutely no brain damage. He was a perfectly normal child who was just a little slow in starting to talk. Since Sri Lanka had no schools for slow learners, the doctors advised us to relocate to the UK and educate him there.

We all enjoyed our tour of Europe at that time and went back home praising God for His faithfulness. It took us five more years to make up our minds to give up everything we had, uproot ourselves, leave all our loved ones and relocate to the UK. We did not see it at that time, but the Lord's hand was on us, opening one door after another. Sarath's job at home offered him a transfer to the head office in London, making the visa a non-issue. We found a buyer for our beautiful home in Sri Lanka, and as I shared previously, the Lord even found us a flat in London for ten days. With our trust in the Lord, we relocated out of a very comfortable and luxurious lifestyle, to a foreign land. Our God is a God of no limits. He supplied all our needs; nothing is impossible for Him. He holds us in the palm of His hand because we are the apple of His eye.

DILIP'S HIP (1975)

It was now about two years since we arrived in the UK, and the enemy struck again. I noticed that Dilip was walking in a strange way but with no complaints of pain. Our GP could not detect what it was but asked us if he played with his brothers, to which we said he did. Dilip had already suffered so much in his short thirteen years of life, all he wanted was to be like his younger brothers.

Since he was a slow learner, the education department decided to place him in a school for children with special needs. As it was in those days, the children had a medical examination annually. When the doctor told me that he was perfect, I mentioned the limp that he was developing. So, she put him back on the couch and then instantly diagnosed Tuberculosis (TB) of the hip. "You have come from a third world country, and it is quite common for children to get TB," she said. She then gave me a letter to my GP asking him to investigate. My GP was quite upset that she had challenged his diagnosis. He felt that there was something wrong with the ankle and had requested an X-ray of it; however, when this came back as normal, he asked me to go to a walk-in clinic for an X-ray of Dilip's hip, which we did.

The next morning, we had a telephone call from Northwick Park Hospital asking us to bring Dilip to a paediatric clinic which was being held that afternoon. We felt the presence of God in the room as soon as we walked in. To our surprise, the consultant immediately asked when we could admit Dilip. No examination, no questions, nothing. All we had was the X-ray.

"Admit him for what?" Sarath and I asked. He then told us that the cartilage in Dilip's hip joint had slipped out and that unless they inserted two pins to hold it in place, he would be in a wheelchair for the rest of his life. Apparently, this happened to one in a million boys at around age thirteen.

Dilip had suffered much but always with a cheerful heart. *How could we explain any of this to our son or his younger brothers?* But we had no choice. Yet what the devil meant for harm the Lord turned it around once more and gave us a testimony. The Lord performed miracle after miracle.

The next day, we packed Dilip a little bag and returned to the hospital. We had no childcare for our other two boys, but the hospital was so kind and understanding that they allowed us all to spend the day in Dilip's room. Apparently, the medical team felt that it would help Dilip if his brothers were with him because this operation was a major one and took time. Dilip was last on the list for surgery. Even during this traumatic time Dilip was amazingly brave—not a tear, not a murmur—all he said was, "It is a shame this has happened to me."

Finally, he was wheeled into theatre at about 2pm. How hard it was for Sarath and I to let go of his little hand; we clung to the Lord for strength and grace. One cannot describe the peace that engulfs a parent as you entrust your child to the Lord. *Jesus, please don't let go of him. Please don't let him feel any pain. Make it quick, Lord. We know You have sent him down to the earth with a great calling on his life. Lord Jesus, please establish Your plans and purposes in his life and keep him safe.*

While Dilip was in theatre, we had a nurse constantly with us, talking to us and comforting us. They could see that we were traumatised. Apparently, the doctor would make a deep cut right up to the thigh bone; they would drill his thigh bone and insert two stainless steel rods of about six inches in length. How heart-breaking it was to listen to all this! But the Lord was with us once again. Even now I cannot believe that we got through this. I kept hearing the words:

Yea, though I walk through the valley of the shadow of death, I will fear no evil; For You are with me; Your rod and Your staff, they comfort me. (Psalm 23:4).

Finally, Dilip was wheeled back to us at about 8pm. Six hours of deep anxiety. Thank God the first step was complete! My husband, Sarath, took the other two boys home and I was allowed to sit in a chair and be with Dilip. All I remember was the dried-up tears on Dilip's cheeks. He kept asking for his brothers, he loved them very much and wanted them with him. We had got through the worst of this nightmare.

I was disappointed with the Lord. *Why did my firstborn have to suffer so much?* At the age of six months, he had Encephalitis and left the hospital having faced death. Now, he was facing this hip problem at age thirteen. Both episodes were classified as one in a million. *Why did You not protect him? He is Your child as well. I am convinced that You have anointed him and sent him to the world for service. Please take care of him.* These were the thoughts that were going through my mind as I sat beside Dilip's bed.

Around midnight, Dilip, in a semiconscious state, said that he needed to pass water. I rang for the nurse who gave me a urinal. She came back after a little while and I told her that he was having difficulty in passing water. "Don't worry," she said, "he has had a great shock to his system. We will send a catheter in the morning. Try to sleep, Dilip."

After she left, I knelt at my son's bed and cried out to the Lord. *"Father please don't let him have to go through any more suffering. Have mercy, Lord! We are in the UK with no friends or family. I can't bear this anymore. No more pain... No more suffering... This is your child. I dedicated him to You at age six months... please, please, help him to pass water."*

I was kneeling at his bed, crying out from the depths of my soul, when suddenly a bright light appeared in the room. It began at the right-hand corner of the ceiling and came down to Dilip's feet. The light was so hot and brilliant, and, in this light, there was what looked like a figure in a white robe. He smiled at us, travelled very slowly above Dilip's little body, and then went away again. I felt led to take out the bottle from under Dilip's sheets, and, to my surprise, the bottle was full! Dilip and I both cried, we both laughed. *Who was that figure? Oh, my Lord! I love You. Was it You, Lord? Was it an angel? I do not know but in my distress, I called out to You, and You answered me.*

Call to Me, and I will answer you...
(Jeremiah 33:3)

Through the storm the joy of Jesus Christ fills us and enables us to be whole. God is light; in Him there is no darkness. Hallelujah! After a week or so, we left the hospital, my son was in crutches, but we were so relieved and happy.

After eighteen months had passed, we had to have another operation to remove the two pins. My husband and I cried. We asked, "If we refuse to sign the consent forms, what will happen?"
"Should there be a car accident or an accident whilst playing, and Dilip should break his bone, it would be very difficult to get at the pins," the consultant explained.

So, after a great deal of discussion, and persuasion, we agreed to the operation. Our hearts were breaking, *how could we let our child go through so much pain?* I continued to cry out to the Lord. *"Nothing is too hard for You, Lord. You are a good God; a miracle worker and You can stop this operation. Please, please, Lord, remove these pins miraculously. I promise to shout from every mountain top and give You all the glory."*

I worked in a psychiatric hospital and my boss even arranged for me to have a chat with one of the consultants because I kept on saying that my God is the God of the impossible and that He could and does do miracles. The psychiatrist laughed at me, but I told him that I knew my God and that He could do the impossible. I believe they thought I was having a nervous breakdown.

Finally, the day of the operation arrived (July 1st, 1977). We took Dilip to hospital, and he was so trusting. I comforted him as best I could, promising that Jesus would never leave him alone. Dilip was 15 years old. We did not know what to expect, but after what seemed like a long time, but was actually only two hours, he was wheeled out of theatre.

The Lord had performed a miracle, but not the way I expected. Dilip came back seated on the bed, full of smiles saying he does not feel any pain and was holding the two pins in his hand. Jesus did not let us down. He sees everything, He was holding Dilip in His arms. He knows what is best for us, He loves us, He sees our tears, and sends us grace from His throne room. He is always there, never leaves us, nor forsakes us.

Dilip's recovery was quick.

A few weeks later, we were on holiday in Devon and whilst watching the boys play —Dilip still with crutches — our hearts were moved. We watched as the two younger brothers cared for their older brother. We did not want him to be a burden on them. In our ignorance, we started discussing the future, "Should we put some money in a trust fund to take care of Dilip's future?" Suddenly, I heard the Lord say, *"Is that all you can trust Me for? He is Mine and I have a plan for his life."* Immediately, we stopped making our plans, repented, and said, *"Lord we surrender Dilip to You, and we will live one day at a time."*

Jesus has been faithful. He is a God of abundance, God of multiplication, He has said, *"My grace is sufficient in your weakness.[2]"* He owns all the silver and the gold, He created all things, He walks with us but never forces Himself on us. What an awesome God He is, so gentle, so forgiving, so loving; the High Priest, the Great I Am, the Almighty, the all-sufficient God of plan and purpose.

---

[2] 2 Corinthians 12:9

God is sovereign. He knows everything. His plans are perfect. Dilip had to have the pins taken out and we cannot tell God how He should do things. He does it the best way. Jesus never deserted us. He was with us through every storm that we faced. How true and absolute is His word? He truly reveals His Father heart to His children. The love of an earthly father is nothing compared to God's love for us. I marvel at His immense, immeasurable love. Glory to God.

EMPLOYMENT

At age sixteen, Dilip had to leave school with no job prospects. As I have mentioned before, when Dilip entered school in England, in 1973, we were informed that we had come too late. Had we come when he was younger, it would have been different.

The next hurdle was finding him a job. The careers office wanted to place him as a gardener or dish washer somewhere, which we knew Dilip would not enjoy. The favour of God had given me a good job which put me in touch with all the heads of departments in the hospital where I worked, so I appealed to all these people for help. God had gone before me and one of these managers said that he would create a job for us and that is what he did.

After a few weeks of leaving school, Dilip started work as a theatre sterilising assistant. He did this for seven years, and his dad, who was an accountant, directed him to handle his personal finances. He gave his tithes to God, gave pocket money to his younger brothers, saved up for holidays and the rest he put in his savings. At the age of twenty-three, he had enough savings to put down as a deposit for a flat. Hallelujah!

After seven years of this job, Dilip felt it was time to move on again. Once again, the Lord was waiting for Dilip to say yes. This time we saw an advert in the paper for a civilian security officer at the Ministry of Defence which was a civil service job with all the benefits. With just one interview and no experience, he was appointed to the job. The favour of God was once more upon his life.

The pension he had accrued at the NHS was transferred to the civil service and he had an unbroken pensionable service. All praise, glory, and honour to God. During this time, unbeknown to us, the Holy Spirit was also teaching Dilip to read and write! The baby who left hospital with the prognosis that he would not talk, see, nor hear, and be in a vegetative state for the rest of his life has today grown up to be of great stature. He drives his own car, owns his own home, and is married to Lakshmie, a girl chosen by God. Above all, he loves the Lord.

GOD'S UNCONDITIONAL LOVE

Around the first week of September 1996, I had a most distressing encounter with a huge being. He was standing beside my bed, about eight feet tall, as black as black can be. He resembled what some may call a giant, a beast from another world. The time was around 2am. He was so ugly, filthy, large, and the only words I can use to describe him was that he was the devil himself. He was carrying my youngest son away, which distressed me immensely, and I cried out to Jesus.

The next two nights were even more horrific. I dreamt I was in this awful battle with Satan. It was so real. "GET OUT OF MY LIFE IN THE NAME OF JESUS CHRIST!" I screamed. My husband woke me up on both occasions and I was still screaming at Satan. These three consecutive nights were most distressing, and it had me confused, wondering if I had grieved the Holy Spirit in any way. I felt anxious and kept thinking that I had separated myself from the Lord. But amazingly, this creature, whom I will refer to as the angel of death, no sooner than he heard the name of Jesus, dropped my son and fled from the scene. Hallelujah! Praise God for His wonderful name.

About a week later, I had another dream. I was at the Wembley Conference Centre with my family attending a meeting where the speaker was a leading evangelist. I was amazed that this speaker recognised us and came to speak with us. We were honoured at first but later felt embarrassed because we thought that we were attracting too much attention. I took the opportunity to share everything that had gone on in our lives and all the miracles that Jesus had performed, but nothing seemed to surprise him. "I know all that," he kept saying.

I was astonished that he knew everything about us. "Thank you for your interest in us," I said to him. "You should probably go and mingle with the other leaders."

"I want to be with you," he replied. "I will never leave you."

I was so honoured and yet perplexed. This was Thursday, September 19th. I woke up in the morning and during my time with the Lord, I asked Him what that dream was all about. Jesus told me that the person I had been talking to was in fact Him and not the evangelist.

That same afternoon, we had to admit our youngest son to hospital. The diagnosis was acute pancreatitis. The doctors spoke to us and said that he was seriously ill, but should he survive, he would be in hospital for at least six to eight weeks. They felt that we should prepare ourselves for the worst. We were extremely shocked and unable to believe what we were hearing, but thank God, He gave us immense strength to cope. His grace was sufficient, and His strength was with us in our weakness.

Our son knew of Jesus at that time but not as his personal saviour. Our primary concern was that if his time on the earth was over, that he would go to our Lord and Father in Heaven. We spoke to him and said that we loved him very much and would pray with all the faith we had for the Lord Jesus to touch him and heal him. "Jesus loves you even more than we love you. Do you believe in Jesus?"

"Of course, I do," he replied.

"Jesus is waiting for you to ask Him to forgive you for neglecting your walk with Him, and to ask Him for healing. That is all it takes. He is a loving Father. If you do that, I guarantee you that you will walk out of this room perfectly whole."

We left him that night with a very heavy heart, but, somehow, we knew that the Lord's hand was upon us all. I knew that no harm would come upon us without the Lord's knowledge. We prayed, took authority over the forces of darkness, and left the rest to the Lord.

> *This is the thing which I have spoken to Pharaoh. God has shown Pharaoh what He is about to do. (Genesis 41:28)*

I now realised the significance of my dreams. I thank God for the advance warning and also for giving me the opportunity to wrestle with Satan in the name that is higher than any other name. I knew that I had the spiritual weapons: the blood of Jesus and the name of Jesus! Weapons of the Kingdom of Heaven to which I belong. I had a peace in my spirit and knew that everything would be alright.

When we visited our son that afternoon. I asked him if he had repented and asked Jesus to heal him. When he said that he had, I assured him that he would be well again. Yet, that evening, everything went horribly wrong, and he became even more ill. We left him that evening with great sadness.

That night, when we went to bed, I heard Jesus tell me that it was not the time to sleep. I knew that the enemy was attacking my son and fighting for my son's life. I telephoned the hospital; it was now 11pm. I was told that there were three doctors with him and that they were doing all they could; they were giving him oxygen in addition to all the other tubes that were already in him.

Jesus and I were engaged in many conversations that night. He asked me to sow a seed in the form of a prayer for another mother who was in the same predicament as I was. The Lord brought a Hindu lady to my mind. I had met her whilst I had been serving coffee and ministering to people at a drop-in centre. She had walked in asking for prayer for her son who was going in for a brain tumour operation; he happened to be the same age as my son. This lady had just lost her husband and now she was told that her son had a very short time to live as well. My heart went out to her, I could feel her pain. When she came to me for prayer, I explained the gospel to her and told her about the love of God for her. I assured her that her son would live if only she would trust and believe in this good news.

Now, in the hour when my son needed healing, the Lord was asking me to stand in the gap for this lady and pray for the healing of her son. I had many healing videos from some of the most famous evangelists, and that night I watched them, and they stirred up my faith. I gave Jesus a list of all the organs of my son which were pronounced dead after the doctors examined the scans. *"Lord, while You're at it, please give him a new heart as well,"* I added. Finally, at around 3am, the Lord said, *"I have heard your prayer, it is done, now go to bed."*

The next morning, I telephoned about six Christian friends, that were firm believers in the Lord, and asked them to agree with me in prayer for my son's complete healing. I did not tell them what the doctors had said because I did not want any unbelief to creep into our prayers. All I told them was that my son was extremely ill in hospital. We agreed that God the healer had him covered, and was on the case, and we were expecting nothing but the impossible. Praise God!

It was only then that one of them said, "Norma, like Abraham did with Isaac, you must be willing to let your son go." This was very hard to hear but I had to do it. *"Lord, Your will be done,"* I said. *"If it is our son's time to go to You, please take him to Your bosom, but please give us the grace to bear this loss."*

It was a very sad sight that awaited us at the hospital. My son was so ill that Sarath and I found it so sad to watch him. We were staring at death but believing for the impossible. Nevertheless, our Lord was with us, comforting us, and upholding us. Even though we were walking through the valley of the shadow of death and darkness, Jesus never left our side nor was our son in too much pain. The Lord was taking the pain way.

Around noon, I heard the Lord say, *"You have informed the elders and the believers, now lay hands on him and take authority over the spirit of death and sickness."* So, my husband and I laid our hands on him straightaway and commanded Satan to leave him. "Be healed in the name of Jesus Christ of Nazareth!"

Within five minutes, he removed the oxygen and said that he could now breathe. He even wanted us to go to the cafeteria and eat some lunch. When we got back, he was a completely different person. He had sat up and moved himself to the chair beside his bed with all the tubes attached to him. "I feel so much better," he said. "I want to go home and rest."

But before we could do that, the registrar came to see him (even though it was a Saturday afternoon). He was truly amazed at the progress my son had made. The doctor even suggested to feed him some semi solid food intravenously on Monday.

On Monday, they were so amazed that they removed all the tubes, instead of putting in more tubes, and they asked me to bring a glass of water for my son to sip. One teaspoon at a time, they had him sip on the water to see if he could retain it, as they expected him to throw up. However, we rebuked what was said by the doctor in the name of Jesus, and, to everybody's amazement, he drank the entire glass of water! They then gave him some soup and jelly for lunch which was also retained.

"He can have a light meal tomorrow," the doctor said. But instead of the light meal, my son amazed them all by eating roast lamb, roast potato and two vegetables! "We don't see any need for him to remain in the hospital. You can take him home," the doctor said. But now the doubts came flooding in and I refused to take him home.
"Why not, Mrs Alahendra?" the doctor asked me. "There are stairs in the house," I replied, as that was the only excuse I could think of. "Two days ago, you told us to expect the worst because he was so

seriously ill but now you want me to take him home." So, they decided to take another scan of his liver, gall bladder, spleen, and pancreas, to see what damage had been done to these organs. To their amazement these organs were absolutely normal, and he was discharged on Friday. Hallelujah! Jesus had answered our prayer by replacing the dead organs with brand new ones.

We give all the glory to our Lord for this wonderful, amazing miracle. When I prayed that night, I asked God for complete healing and new organs for the damaged ones that showed in the first scan. As I saw in that vision, our Lord knows everything, but He waits for us to seek His face and ask Him for whatever we need. I know that He is alive; every word in the book of life, the Bible, is a living word. It is so packed with life, I pray daily for more revelation and understanding. Jesus is alive; He died for all mankind. He loves us all. He is our Friend, our Redeemer, our Lord, and our God. Oh! That we might know Him even deeper.

Thank You, Lord, for loving me. Thank You, Lord, that You know everything about us. Thank You, Jesus, that we do not need to do anything but only believe Your Word. There is nothing that we have to do to earn Your love. It is a free gift available to anyone who believes in the Lord Jesus Christ. Amen and amen.

Chapter 7

LAMPLUGH HOUSE IN YORKSHIRE

One Sunday morning, in 1988, our vicar informed the congregation that he was organising a five-day retreat to Lamplugh House in Yorkshire. The retreat was to be held in December that year, and he invited those of us who were interested to book our places. I had never gone away on my own before and was rather apprehensive; nevertheless, I felt the prompting of the Holy Spirit, so I put my name down.

It was a cold wintery morning when the retreat finally came around. There were nine of us making the journey, and we reached Yorkshire in the early evening. It was most uninviting; dark, snowing heavily, and the temperature must have been below zero. My initial reaction was fear. *What am I doing here, away from my family?* I felt so alone, very uncomfortable. I felt like I needed to escape but there was no way out.

In addition to our church group, there were also about thirty to forty people arriving from various other churches. We were allocated our rooms and already God had gone ahead of me and seen to it that I had a bedroom to myself. The other participants were all discussing what their favourite books of the Bible were and what they were expecting to receive from the week. All the while, I was getting even more uncomfortable, and all my insecurities were coming to the surface. *"Father God, I am at a loss, I don't belong here, I'm sure I have made a mistake. I am not meant to be here. The others here are very mature Christians. But, God, You know all this, Your favour is upon me."*

He had allocated a room just for me, while most of the others had to share. At least I could be alone in my room. What an amazing God we serve! He loves us and He will never embarrass us. He showed me that He brought me there to teach me His purposes, His love, His mercy, and His grace. What an awesome God He is. I wanted to escape but God had brought me to a place from which there was no escape. He was saying to me, *"My grace is sufficient for you, for My strength is made perfect in weakness."* (2 Corinthians 12:9).

After a cup of tea, we unpacked and assembled for a time of worship. This was amazing; a group of like-minded people who all wanted the same thing, to meet with God our Master, Saviour, Redeemer, and Deliverer. God has no favourites; He knows each one of us intimately; He was going to have His way. He created us, He moulded us and had brought us there for a purpose in order to fulfil His plans. He loved us and He wanted to reveal His love, compassion, and grace. He was getting His army ready.

After worship, we went for dinner and were informed that, during the retreat, we were not to have any conversations with anyone else except the leadership. The focus of the retreat was about looking only unto God — upwards and forwards. It was beautiful. The atmosphere was so peaceful, serene, and wonderful. I looked forward to the times of worship and also the teaching and meditation. We were all tired and slept well and woke up refreshed and ready for whatever the Lord had planned for us.

On the second evening, when we had retired to our rooms, I was on my knees beside my bed, in deep conversation with the Lord. *"Lord, You know everything about me. I feel so inadequate, all my insecurities are being exposed; I have no idea why You brought me here, I do not know the Scriptures like the others do. Can You use me? Would You please teach me? I must know for sure that You can use me to fulfil your purposes."*

Unfortunately, while I was in this form of prayer, I heard someone knock on my door. I was naive enough to ask the Lord to forgive me for leaving my prayer time and went to the door. But when I opened the door, there was no one there. So, I got back on my knees once more. Then another knock disturbed my deep conversation with the Lord, and once again, I went to the door, but nobody was there.

I plucked up courage to knock on my neighbour's door, "Did you knock on my door?"
"No," they replied.
So, once more, I came back to my room, got on my knees, and this time, after apologising to the Lord, I was determined to spend some good quality time with Him. I was pleading with the Lord, telling Him that I had to know that He wanted me there. *"Lord, do You need me? Do You love me? Am I forgiven for my past sins?*

Then for the third time, I heard the same knock at my door; however, this time I smiled and asked, *"Jesus, is that You? You came to Samuel, the little boy, and called him three times, is it possible that this could be a sign? An answer to my questions... Have You orchestrated this retreat purely to get my attention? Oh, thank You, Father! Thank You for Your love; Your mercy; Your grace."*

The Scriptures say:

> *"Let us therefore come boldly to the throne of grace, that we may obtain mercy and find grace to help in time of need."* (Hebrews 4:16)

I was so happy and so at peace with God because He was meeting with me and speaking to me.

The next morning, at breakfast, we were told that if we needed any questions answered we could put our names down to make an appointment to talk to one of the leaders. I had always had a problem with speaking in tongues, so I put my name down and ended up receiving counsel from a bishop who had so much compassion and love oozing out of him. He listened to me and spoke to me for a while, and then laid hands on me and prayed. I was baptised with the Holy Spirit that day, and, very hesitantly, began my journey of speaking and praying in tongues. What I remember most was the peace that engulfed me. The joy was immense, so much so that I did not want to go back home, I wanted to remain on that mountaintop forever. I could sense the Lord transforming me from within. His love was overwhelming. I had no doubt that God would use me if I said yes. I was gradually coming back to where He wanted me to be. He was simply waiting for me to say that I wanted to serve Him. The Father heart of God was being revealed to me. Nothing was too much for Him, His hand was upon me. He loved me.

> *"My son, give me your heart, And let your eyes observe my ways." (Proverbs 23:26)*

> *"Let us draw near with a true heart in full assurance of faith, having our hearts sprinkled from an evil conscience and our bodies washed with pure water." (Hebrews 10:22)*

God was beckoning me. I loved Him; I was seeking Him with all of my heart. It was just God and me. He had my full attention, no distractions of family and home.

Alas! By the end of the week, the retreat came to an end; we got onto the coach and embarked on the long journey back home. We had a wonderful time of praise and worship on the coach, the Lord loved it too. About three hours of loving Him and being ministered to by Him. We arrived back to London late that evening where my children came running to greet me. I embraced each one of them and told them how much I loved them. They could sense a change in me. Yes, the Lord was transforming me, and I knew it too. He put a deep hunger in me for Him. I was filled with such love for Him. Nothing but the Lord could satisfy me. Each one of us that embarked on that journey to Lamplugh House had met with our Saviour in the way that the Lord had planned it. Hallelujah! Glory to God! Thank You, Jesus. Amen.

Chapter 8

LIFE AFTER LAMPLUGH HOUSE (ROFFEY PLACE)

Having returned from the retreat, the Lord was drawing me closer to Him. I was studying the Word voraciously, seeking Him, offering myself in any way that I could to the church leadership: leading Bible studies, doing The Alpha Course, distributing communion, and taking part in the preparations for baptisms. These are some of the ministries I took part in. As time passed, I felt the need to study further. I knew I could not stop where I was.

I kept seeking the Lord and looking for somewhere I could go to study and learn more about discipleship and servanthood. With much prayer and seeking the Lord, I ended up at Kingdom Faith Bible School in Roffey Place, Horsham. It was a one-year residential course in discipleship which changed me completely. I realised it was not what I could do for God but what He was calling me to do. *What was His plan for me? What had He prepared for me even before He formed me in my mother's womb?* When you step into God's plan, He arranges all things, and you only have to make yourself available to Him.

> *"For we are His workmanship, created in Christ Jesus for good works, which God prepared beforehand so that we would walk in them." (Ephesians 2:10)*

He will equip you to step into His plans. No striving because He does the work through You.

> *"... 'Not by might nor by power, but by My Spirit,' says the LORD of armies." (Zechariah 4:6)*

By faith, I accepted that Almighty God had put me into Christ at Calvary. I learnt who I was in Christ. I was crucified with Christ; it was no longer I who lived but Christ who lived in me (Galatians 2:20). Though my sins were as scarlet, He washed me whiter than snow. I died with Him, was buried with Him, and rose again when Christ rose from the dead. I am a new creature in Christ, God's own creation. The old person died, I am now washed in the blood of Jesus, sinless, born of the Word and the Spirit of God. The child that was born to my parents no longer exists.

Jesus answered and said to him, "Most assuredly, I say to you, unless one is born again, he cannot see the kingdom of God." (John 3:3)

"Jesus said to him, 'I am the way, the truth, and the life. No one comes to the Father except through Me.'" (John 14:6)

Our first evening at Roffey Place was an eye-opener. Pastor Colin welcomed us and then said he would pass the microphone around to each student so that we could share why we had come to college. "God would have spoken to each of you and given you a specific reason as to why He has sent you here," Pastor Colin said. "If you do not yet know why you are here, then now is the time to ask Him. John 10:27 says, *'My sheep hear My voice and they follow Me'*. God speaks to His children all the time, so ask Him why He has brought you here."

I panicked when I heard all this, but, in that state of panic, I had to get quiet. *"Please, Lord, I have to have an answer,"* I prayed. To my complete surprise, I actually heard Him deep within my spirit. He said, *"I have given you the time, provided the funds, now learn of Me, and go and teach others and make disciples and not just converts. Teach those that*

*want to learn but don't have the time or the funds.
Freely you have received freely give."*

Due to ill health, I had retired at the age of forty-five after I suffered a heart attack and was left with heart problems. The Lord gave me wisdom to invest in stocks and shares which made enough money for both me and Sarath to pay the board and lodgings for the course at Roffey Place. So, here we were, with time and money which God had provided. Isn't it wonderful how the Lord had thought of every last detail? Sarath had also taken early retirement for no apparent reason, so we closed up our home in London and travelled to West Sussex where we began our journey. Such love, amazing love. He is the Alpha and Omega, the Creator of the universe, the Ancient of Days, the Great I Am. Full of wisdom, slow to anger, abounding in grace.

I had been walking about with so much guilt and shame, but my Lord had once again brought me to the right place. The more I heard about God's grace, the more freedom I experienced. I felt so liberated. The joy, the elation, was beyond words. Yes, the Scriptures say we have to grow in our salvation, and God opened my heart to receive His Word by faith. *Jesus, I love You; how wonderful you are. I am free. I am free of the guilt and shame of my past. Such love, such mercy.*

As the song written by Bill Gaither's says:

> *"He touched me, Oh He touched me,*
> *And oh the joy that floods my soul!*
> *Something happened and now I know,*
> *He touched me and made me whole."*

Each day that I spent at Roffey was an eye opener. God kept revealing His love for me. Day by day, Jesus was satisfying my hunger, my desire for Him. He kept wooing me, beckoning me ever closer to Him. My first love for Him was being rekindled. That bridal love was becoming more and more real and intense. He was doing all the work in me, all I had to do was trust Him and obey Him. I needed to trust Him while He gently kept transforming me. It was a wonderful time of loving and being loved by my Saviour, my Lord, my Redeemer, my God. How amazing is my God? So patient, so understanding.

I kept encountering my God, my King, the Lord, the Miracle Worker, the Promise Keeper, the Light in the darkness. I was being drawn to His Word. He is the Way, the Truth, and the Life. He was showing me how much He loved me. He is so faithful, so dependable, so patient. He is my Rock, the Anchor to my soul, the Chief Cornerstone. This relationship sometimes seems so one-sided; He does not ask much from us, only that we believe and trust Him. Just like a child would trust and believe his earthly father.

He is my Peace, my Joy, my Wisdom, my Companion, my all in all. This is what is available to each one of us. He has no favourites; His love for His children is the same. As a mother of three, I know that I cannot favour one child more than the other. How much more does He yearn to pour out His love on each one of His children. What a Father!

While at Roffey we had a few visiting teachers scheduled to talk to us students. Some carried the prophetic anointing, others had healing anointings, and so on. I watched them prophesy over some students and began envying the students who had received a word of prophecy. I would envy them and wish that someone would encourage me with a word from the Lord. When I asked the Lord about this, I heard Him say to me, *"I have not appointed any of these to give you a word. No man will give you a word, just look to Me and I will speak to you directly. You are My child, and I will guide you."* In fact, He led me to Psalm 23:

"The Lord is my shepherd; I shall not want.
He makes me to lie down in green pastures;
He leads me beside the still waters.
He restores my soul;
He leads me in the paths of righteousness
For His name's sake.

Yea, though I walk through the valley of the
shadow of death, I will fear no evil;
For You are with me;
Your rod and Your staff, they comfort me.

You prepare a table before me in the presence
of my enemies;
You anoint my head with oil;
My cup runs over.
Surely goodness and mercy shall follow me
All the days of my life;
And I will dwell in the house of the Lord
Forever."

One of the first things they taught us at this college was to spend a whole week without using the words 'I', 'me' or 'my' in our conversations. This was not easy, but it was a great way to train us to die to self, to always keep your focus on things above. It was simple but profound.

The Lord was very gentle, He did not frighten us, but He taught us that before we could serve Him, we needed to know Him and love Him. We had to touch the Father heart of God; He is not a harsh judge but a fair and gentle Lord. We needed to approach Him without fear but with reverence. He is our Father, but we had to learn to trust Him, revere Him, and worship Him in spirit and truth. All scripture is God breathed: His Word is truth; His Word is absolute; His Word is like a two-edged sword, sharp pointed. Unless you trust Him, you cannot operate through the Word. God's Word does not return to Him void: if He said it, it will happen — *only believe.*

The times of worship at Roffey were out of this world. I could see Jesus ministering to the others similarly. The Father heart of God is so real, so loving, so gentle. There were times when I felt so close to Him, just Jesus and me. As we basked in His presence, soaking up the atmosphere, we were being transformed from within. At one such meeting, during a time of worship, I felt something going on in my chest. I turned to my husband and said, "I think the Lord is performing surgery on my heart. It feels like there's a sharp knife moving in my chest." No anaesthetics: nevertheless, surgery was being performed. I have not had any trouble with my heart since that day in 1994.

> *"And we know that all things work together for good to those who love God, to those who are the called according to His purpose."* (Romans 8:28)

He moves the pieces of the jigsaw to fit into every circumstance of our life, nothing is wasted.

So much happened in that one year, and we came back home full of excitement but also trepidation and fear. However, one thing I was certain of, no matter what we had to face, our God would take us through it as long as we submitted to Him. He does not force us to do anything we do not want to do, but if we walk with Him, He will open doors for us. If we say no to Him, He will still wait.

LIFE AFTER ROFFEY

When we came back home, we re-joined our church, and met with our vicar to offer our services as part of the congregation. He welcomed us back very warmly and even asked us to start a Bible study in our home; he also asked us to join the prayer ministry team as before. We were joyfully fulfilling our duties, as expected, but unfortunately, other members of the church noticed that there was a change in us and started talking about this change to the leadership. This was not a good thing: the leadership began to change towards us. Nevertheless, we carried on trusting God and obeying Him.

We saw the hunger in some of our friends, they wanted to learn more about the Lord. They were seeking God with a genuine desire to get closer to Him. We heard the Lord tell us to invite one of our teachers from Roffey to come and speak to the congregation, so we approached the church leadership and asked if we could invite Dr John McKay to do this. They agreed and we set about organising this event asking the vicar to be in charge at the event. Unfortunately, a few days before the event, the vicar called us in to his office, and was very rude to us, accusing us of being involved in a cult.

"I do not want anyone from my church to have anything to do with that ministry," the vicar said. We were left in a very embarrassing position because all the plans had already been put in place. Sarath and I knew that the Lord had asked us to organise that meeting; we were so disappointed but had to submit to the leadership of the church.

Thankfully, John, our teacher at that time, had become a very good friend of ours.

"Not to worry," John said when we informed him of our predicament. "I can come to your home instead and talk to anyone who happens to be there."

We were amazed at his humility!

The next morning, Sarath went for his regular walk. As he passed the village community centre, he said he felt compelled to go inside and meet with the caretaker about hiring the hall. He was shown two rooms, one accommodating thirty people and another to seat one hundred.

"I booked and paid for the smaller room," he later told me. "Let's be in faith for the thirty to turn up!"

"Well, the leadership have already given us strict instructions not to introduce any one from Roffey to members of the church," I replied. "So, if we're in faith for thirty people from outside our church, then why don't we believe God for the hundred?"

"You're right," Sarath agreed. So, he went back to the community centre and paid the deposit for the larger room. The two of us then went to the Lord and prayed. *"Here we are Lord, just the two of us and two of our sons. Lord, You send the people. We have booked the larger room in faith believing that You are able to fill this room. So have Your way."*

Finally, the day arrived for the meeting. The four of us got the room ready for one hundred guests and arranged for some friends to lead worship. We held hands and praised God for the wonderful way His name would be glorified. It was His day and nothing and nobody was going to hijack it. When the time for the meeting arrived, a mighty storm broke out with thunder and lightning. Nevertheless, people turned up; the Lord sent them! Some we recognised and some we did not. Our two sons, who had helped us lay out the one hundred chairs, were now standing out in the storm, acting as carpark attendants and later served the teas and coffees — truly it was a family affair. Between the four of us, the meeting was a great success and John's message impacted most of those that attended.

From that first meeting, came the birthing of more meetings. As mentioned previously, our church leadership had no objections to us starting a Bible Study in our home, so we welcomed those who wanted to study the Word to our home on Wednesday evenings at 7:30pm. Again, our Lord surprised us. He always has His way; He is so amazing! Over twenty-five people turned up for Bible study, and these were times of wonderful praise and worship, along with a short message.

These meetings were wonderful but very stressful for me as I had never done anything like this before. I cried most of the time as I prepared those messages. I was so afraid because I was delivering the Word of God which is so precious. However, the Lord had to remind me that He would do the talking so long as I submitted to Him and let Him speak through me.

Faithful to His Word, there were unexpected miracles and healings that took place at these evening meetings. We carried on for a while and the Lord sustained us and protected us. We stood back, amazed at what was taking place, and watched the Lord at work. The power of God was so marvellous, so awe inspiring. We basked in His glory. The way He moved among our friends that assembled in our home was truly breath-taking! The Lord was showing us that it was not who we are that matters but who He is. He can take the weakest person, the most insignificant person and use us for His glory.

He is the Great I Am, the Beginning and the End. The God of gods, The King of kings. He will honour our faith in Him. He says:

> *"I will never leave you nor forsake you."*
> *(Hebrews 13:5)*

"I am with you always." (Matthew 28:20)

"Fear not, for I am with you." (Isaiah 41:10)

"Trust in the LORD, and do good." (Psalm 37:3)

He was showing us His Father heart. He loved these people who were coming into our home and wanted to fill their hunger. They were seeking God and He was showing them His mercy and grace.

After some months had passed, the vicar of our church made inquiries from those who attended our meetings. He wanted to know how they were progressing. Our friends were very enthusiastic and told him that they would like to continue these groups; however, somehow their comments seemed to offend him. We were summoned to the church and told that we should stop hosting our meetings straight away. "It's time you come down from the clouds and live a normal life," we were told. So, with much sadness, we agreed to disband the gatherings knowing that the Lord would open other doors if that was what He wanted.

About that same time, we received a telephone call from a stranger.

"I've heard about your meetings," they said. "I'd really like to attend."

"Unfortunately, we have had to discontinue these meetings," we replied.

"Oh no, really?" the stranger sounded disappointed.

"We can contact you if we restart another group," we said. "Would you like to leave your contact details with us?"

"Yes, definitely that sounds great, thank you," they said and gave us their details.

The Lord is truly amazing! Within a few days we received three similar calls asking us the same question. We believed this had to be God, so we got in touch with each of these callers and asked them which day of the week would suit them best so we could meet up and have a chat. We also asked them what time and day would be most convenient should we restart our meetings.

By now we had about five couples wanting to come. We did not know these couples, and they did not know us, nor did they know each other, but they all lived within a three-mile radius of our home. Monday evenings were the common denominator, so we invited them to our home on Monday at 7pm. There were over a dozen of us seated around our table introducing ourselves to each other and getting to know each other. It seemed so natural. Like-minded people with a hunger to get to know the Almighty, our God and Lord. We had never done anything like this before, opening our home to strangers.

Before Monday, we telephoned our tutor at the Bible School, Dr John McKay, and asked for his help. "We don't know how to proceed," we told him. "We know God is in this but where should we start? What should we do first?"

"It definitely does look like God is in this," he said, "So… what is He telling you to do now?"

I realised I knew what God was saying, "Well, on the first day at Bible School God spoke to me and said, *'I have provided the funds and the time for you to learn; now go out and teach others who do not have the money or the time to go to Bible School and learn of me.'*"

"That's your answer then," John said. "Teach them everything you have learnt."

John had written a Bible study course called "The Way of the Spirit" which we used at Roffey. This course disciplined students to wait on God daily by reading the Word of God and waiting on Him for revelation. It was the study of the New Testament and relevant Old Testament books. When we suggested this course of study to the group, they agreed, and we embarked on this study for the next two years.

These people were so hungry for God. They were so keen and faithful in doing their homework, and in committing to a daily routine of reading, studying the Word of God, and looking forward to receiving a fresh revelation from the Father. They came from many different denominations, but it made no difference to the Lord. They were all part of His body, all Kingdom people, citizens of Heaven. Our Lord was well pleased with each one of them. We began to realise that we were carrying a heavy responsibility; nevertheless, if God had chosen us to lead this group, He would make sure that these, His children, were well fed.

As we look back, we are truly amazed at how the Lord worked. Moving His people around, bringing them together under one roof to study and to learn from Him and each other. Some of them ended up as missionaries, another a pastor. To God be the glory! He gave us the privilege of watching His children being transformed by the Holy Spirit. We sat back and watched the Lord at work. We did nothing. He did the work. What a privilege and an honour. The people who left us were not the same people who came to us. They were transformed, refined and ready for service.

While God was working in those He had entrusted to us, changing them, and getting them ready for service, we were simultaneously facing a lot of persecution from outside. Yet, God remained faithful and taught us how to face and handle spiritual warfare. We saw that the enemy uses people from within the church to discourage us. Family was also used to persecute us. However, the Lord watched over us. He encouraged us and brought us through, and more discipleship groups were birthed in our home by the Lord. Amen!!

Chapter 9

THE VISION OF THE GLORY OF THE LORD

CONSECRATE YOURSELF, FOR I SHALL DO A GREAT WORK IN YOU

I had finished my readings for that morning, shut my Bible, and was meditating on the Word. Suddenly, I heard these words deep in my spirit:

"Consecrate yourself, for I shall do a great work in you."

I was taken aback. *Did I really just hear this instruction, or was it just my own thoughts? What do these words mean?* I decided to forget what I had heard and move on, but somehow, they would not leave me. Again, I heard the same words deep inside me, so I decided to tell my husband.

"Sarath, I heard the Lord speak to me. He told me to consecrate myself; He said He shall do a great work in me. What should I do?"

"We should inquire of the Lord," replied Sarath, and I agreed.

"Lord, please tell me what these words mean," I prayed.

"Consecrate yourself, for I shall do a great work in you." Once more, the Lord was speaking these same words to me.

"Jesus, I do not understand what I am meant to do, so please do whatever it takes. You know that I want to obey You and get closer to You." As I finished those words of prayer, the Lord began to show me some areas in my life that were not glorifying Him, and I had to repent and ask the Holy Spirit to take charge and transform me in every area of my being.

BE HOLY BECAUSE I AM HOLY

The first instructions I had heard from the Lord, came in March of 1995; it was now May. I was happy and yet this frightened me.

"Jesus, what is happening?" I asked the Lord.

"I am in you, and you are in Me; therefore, be Holy because I am Holy," He replied. *"You do not have to do anything, just accept it, and receive it. I have already made you holy."*

Such a calm came upon me. So much peace. I was being transformed by the Lord Himself. He did not expect me to do anything or strive to be holy. It was a time of complete submission to Jesus. Being in His presence, basking in Him, knowing that He was having His way. This went on for some months where I felt the tangible presence of the Lord on me. It was so intense.

About six weeks before Christmas, in 1995, I had such a restlessness in my spirit. I cried out to the Lord to show me something more of Himself, for nothing would satisfy my yearning for Him. I knew that He had said, *"Be Holy because I AM holy"*, and that the Holy Spirit was my enabler, so I asked Him to make me holy so that I may see Jesus. I asked the Lord for the crumbs that were left over from what the disciples had received. I would've been satisfied with even a little of the power that they had received — anything, something — to take me further from where I was at that time.

Gradually, I began to feel a deep yearning for the Lord that I had not known before. The intensity of this yearning, desire, love, whatever we may choose to call it, grew to such a pitch that I said this to my son a few days before Christmas: "I love Jesus so much. Unless He does something to help me, my heart will literally burst open."

The attack of the enemy came at me with a vengeance on Christmas day. Around lunch time I was taken ill, and the family meal was ruined. We recognised the attack of the evil one and immediately took authority over him and rebuked him in the name of Jesus. Thankfully, after a couple of hours rest, I was able to re-join the family for a meal.

That night, I slept peacefully but woke up feeling exhausted. The doctor visited me the next evening and said that he believed I had had a mild heart attack. "If you feel bad tonight, you *must* go to hospital," the doctor said.

The night of December 26th (1995) was very uncomfortable. I was unable to sleep and felt quite unwell, so I began a conversation with Jesus. *"Lord, I know that sickness is not of You because You took our infirmities with You to the cross,"* I said. *"I recognise that this is the attack of the enemy; he has come to steal what You are doing, and to destroy whatever wonderful thing that is about to take place. But why is it that, even after taking authority over the devil and rebuking him, I still feel unwell?"*

Jesus had provided for my husband and I to attend Bible school, to teach us so much, and yet, something that I was doing was not right.

"Lord, if my time on the earth is over, please take me home without allowing Satan to have a hand in it."

"You shall not see death," that was God's promise to me.

Even whilst I was talking with the Lord, I felt myself leaving my body, through my ear, travelling at the speed of light. I heard something like loud peels of thunder: it was like a mighty fireworks display. The sound was majestic but deafening, and yet so awesome. I was transported in this container, something like a cable car and there was a great light around it. I saw separate colourful galaxies (green, pink, yellow, blue, purple).

I found myself in this great light. There was no tunnel, no beam of light, I was in the light: gleaming white light, amazing, brilliant light. I saw no one but I was in the light.

Then I heard a roar of a mighty thunder and brilliant white lightning, accompanied with the sound of many orchestras — thousands of them. I could hear the sound of many harps, stringed instruments. Oh! it was so majestic, so awesome! I wish I could find words to describe what I saw.

Along with this, I heard the roar of a great multitude of voices, thousand upon thousand; ten thousand upon ten thousand, worshipping the Lord in unison and perfect harmony. I was in the centre of all that was going on, worshipping and praising the Lord with everything within me, with all my heart and soul. It was so loud and yet so majestic, so magnificent, so beautiful, so awesome.

From this light, that we were all in, I saw the map of the world down below. It was in complete darkness; every detail was there, every little island was visible, but the world was in complete darkness.

I now became aware of how loud my praises were and that I might be disturbing my husband who was asleep beside me. Immediately, I felt myself re-entering my body, and was amazed that I was still praising God, but I was not making any sound at all, just praising Him in silence and in tongues. Once again, I felt myself leave and get back into that awesome glory. It was even more majestic and more holy.

Now the map of the world had tiny dots of brilliant light scattered around in many of the countries. We continued singing praises to our God, and suddenly, in a flash, there was something like a magnificent display of fireworks and all parts of the world began to light up. At first it was slow, then it became faster until the whole world was engulfed in the light. I knew that Satan had tried to steal, kill and destroy something but Jesus revealed His glory! I beheld His glory, His wonderful, amazing glory. I wish I knew how or had the words to truly describe what I saw.

While I was in this glory, something I noticed was that every thought I had was being answered. It was as though my thoughts were being answered by a higher being; communication was by thought transference. I noticed that I was right in the centre of this glory!

"How can this be?" I thought to myself. *"I am just a small being in this vast Kingdom."*

"All My children are equal in My Kingdom," the Lord's answer immediately came back to me. *"As a hen gathers her chicks, so I gather My children. I love you all the same."*

I understood that the Lord meant we are all at the centre of His love; we are all the apple of His eye.

Finally, the whole earth was being covered with His glory. The world that I had seen below, which was once covered in a thick darkness, was now being revealed in brilliant white light! Jesus is ALIVE. He will have His way. What a mighty God we serve. He heard and answered me. He is a faithful God who never leaves us. He carries us through times of trials and tribulations. Hallelujah! Amen.

DECEMBER 2000

One day as I sat meditating on all that the Lord had done for me, through me, and deep within me, I heard the Lord say, *"You cannot praise me from the grave after I have called you home to Me. Write your testimonies down so that others may know and experience what I have done for and through you. All who call on Me and come to Me are mine. I love My children, all My children. I have no favourites. I am God."*

How can someone write down all that God is? There is so much more that Jesus has done for me and my family. I have tried to convey to you:

1. The Father heart of God: His unconditional love, mercy, grace and power.

2. The love of Jesus, the Servant King, and yet the King of kings. He longs to take us to Almighty God who is His Father. He is the Good Shepherd. He said, *"My sheep hear My voice, and I know them, and they follow Me"* (John 10:27). He is Emmanuel, God with us. The Prince of Peace, the Light of the world. The Miracle Worker, the Healer, Deliverer, Messiah, Saviour.

3. The transforming power of the Holy Spirit who comes to dwell in us, changes us from within, and then uses us for the glory of God.

Jesus is the only way to the Father. He took me, a sinner, and forgave me completely; He put a robe of righteousness on me though my sins were as scarlet. He washed me whiter than snow by the redeeming power of His blood. He has now offered me everlasting life, life in abundance forever more. He is my Rock, the Anchor of my soul; He is faithful, never changing. He is Sovereign; His Word is truth and never comes back void.

If you have never invited Him into your heart just do so now. Tell Him you believe in Him, and you want Him to be your Lord. He loves you and waits with open arms to receive you.

ACKNOWLEDGEMENTS

I would like to thank a few people who have helped me to put this book together: My granddaughter Melina, my son Nihal, and my son Dilip and his wife, Lakshmie. I also want to thank my friend Amanda McCaskie.

"The angel of the Lord encamps all around those who fear Him, and delivers them."

—Psalm 34:7